Diet recommendations for esophageal carcinoma

Please check these recommendations always with a nutrition consultant, therapist, doctor or dietician. The recipes and the list of ingredients are supporting the conventional medical therapy.
The calorie disclosures of fresh ingredients (fruit and vegetables) vary according to quality and time of harvest. The contents were checked by a dietician and a nutrition consultant for the Traditional Chinese Medicine (TCM).

Author:
©2017 Josef Miligui
www.ebns.at

AF2208867

Source:
The lists are created from the EBNS database for nutritional counseling. The database is used by dietitians, therapists and doctors for advising the patient / client.

Literature:
The specialist literature and the training documents of the German and Austrian dietary and traditional Chinese medicine serve as a knowledge base. We have used the documents as a basis of knowledge, adapted it to our experience and completed them.
http://di-book.com

Title Photo:
©2008 Erika Weixlbaumer

Production and publishing:
BoD – Books on Demand, Norderstedt
ISBN: 9783752861518

Diet recommendations for DIETETICS - Mouth and esophagus - Esophageal carcinoma

1   Treatment strategy

Directed to the condition.
Light normal diet. Anti-inflammatory teas (eg: chamomile, sage).
Avoid food with a coarse structure.
Fruit acid containing fruit and drinks such as orange, lemon or grapefruit juice and fruit teas can cause additional pain.
Also the use of ready-made baby food in the glass is useful in the individual case, since this is very mildly seasoned.

2   Avoid

Rusks, crispbread, semolina or milk rice, orange, lemon or grapefruit juice, fruit teas.
Caution: Acid-containing food and drink, Salty foods, Strongly flavored foods, Alcohol.
Too hot dishes.

3 Breakfast

4 Snack

5 Lunch

6   Afternoon

7   Dinner

8   Any time

9 Recipes

(recommendable) = You can use more.
(little) = You should use less than specified or omit.

9.1 Adzuki Bean and Rice Soup

Strengthens spleen, heart, kidney and stomach, supports urination, improves blood circulation, reduces inflammation.
Cooking time approx. 2 hours
Calories p. portion: 199
1 portions
Allergens:

Quantity of ingredients:
Adzuki beans 8 table spoons / 40g. (yes)
Rice round grain 2 table spoons / 20g. (yes)
Water 1 1/2 cups / 200g. (yes)
Honey 1 table spoon / 8g. (recommended)

Cooking instructions:
Boil soaked adzuki beans and round grain rice in a ratio of 4: 1 in water until a thin pulp has formed. Sweet as needed; possibly puree.

Effect: This recipe strengthens kidney, spleen and stomach and is particularly suitable for mothers with too little milk flow.

9.2 Apple - banana cream

Regulates gastrointestinal function, provides vitamin C, cholesterol lowering, reduces inflammation, diuretic, improves blood circulation.
Cooking time approx. 15 min
Calories p. portion: 110
4 portions
Allergens:

Quantity of ingredients:
Apple (sour) 7/8 lbs / 400g. (recommended)
Water 3/4 cup - 6 oz / 200g. (yes)
Orange peel 1/4 piece / 5g. (yes)
Lemon peel 1/2 piece / 2g. (yes)
Sugar brown 2 teaspoons / 6g. (recommended)
Cinnamon sticks 1 piece / 0g. (yes)
Banana 1 piece / 150g. (yes)

Acerola fruit nectar or powder 1 teaspoon / 2g. (yes)
Orange juice 1/2 piece / 50g. (recommended)
Lemon juice 1 table spoon / 10g. (yes)

Cooking instructions:
Cut the apple into fine slices, bring water to boil and add the apple slices, orange- and lemon peel, sugar and cinnamon and simmer about 7 minutes. The apples should be almost soft. Remove acerola and the cinnamon stick.
Mix the apple, the banana, the orange juice and the lemon juice.

9.3   Apple sauce with raisins

Stops diarrhea, promotes digestion, appetizing, relieves diarrhea, activates carbohydrate metabolism.
Cooking time approx. 25 min
Calories p. portion: 74
10 portions
Allergens: O

Quantity of ingredients:
Apple (sweet) 2,2 lbs / 1000g. (recommended)
Water 1/2 cup / 100g. (yes)
Raisins 1/8 lbs - 2oz / 50g. (yes)

Cooking instructions:
Wash, peel and quarter the apples and remove the core. Put the apples with the water in a pot. Wash the raisins with hot water and add them. Cook at low heat for about 10 minutes, then allow to cool. Crush with the potato steamer. Fill and seal in a freezer or empty yoghurt jug. Close the yoghurt jug. Freeze in the shock freezer.
If necessary, thaw at room temperature for about 6 hours. (Lasting about 4 months).
The fruit mousse is intended as dessert or intermediate meal. It has an anti-digestive effect. In case of diarrhea give better banana.

9.4   Apricot and cranberry ice cream

Forces resistance to infections, good to fight oral mucosal inflammation, diarrhea. Has a positive effect on the urinary tract.
Cooking time approx. 5 min
Calories p. portion: 106
2 portions
Allergens:

Quantity of ingredients:
Apricots 3/4 lbs / 350g. (yes)
Water 1/4 cup / 50g. (yes)
Cranberry 2 table spoons / 45g. (yes)

Cooking instructions:
Mix the apricot juice with the cranberry syrup. Fill the juice into little molds, place in the freezer and let it freeze in about 3 hours.

9.5 Banana porridge

Regulates gastrointestinal function. Protects the digestive system. Detoxifying, affects anorexia, good to fight flatulence, inflammatory bowel disease.
Cooking time approx. 10 Min
Calories p. portion: 235
1 portions
Allergens: AG

Quantity of ingredients:
Water 1/2 cup / 125g. (yes)
Wheat flakes 1/2 oz / 20g. (yes)
Banana 1/4 lbs - 4oz / 100g. (yes)
Butter organic 1 table spoon / 10g. (yes)

Cooking instructions:
Mix the water with the flakes in a small pan. Bring to boil by low heat, cook for 1-2 minutes and then remove from the cooking area. Cut the banana in pieces into the pot, add the butter and puree with a blender. Fill the banana porridge into a plate.
Instead of butter, you can also take corn oil - especially when the porridge is not so hot, the oil is distributed more easily.
If you use buckwheat, millet, corn or rice flakes instead of wheat flakes, the mash is gluten-free.

9.6 Banana Soymilk

Good to fight loss of appetite, oral mucosa inflammation. Strengthens body energy, promotes stomach-spleen harmony, promotes digestion, regulates gastrointestinal function. Relieves pain, detoxifying, bactericide.
Cooking time approx. 5 min
Calories p. portion: 126

2 portions
Allergens: E

Quantity of ingredients:
Banana 1 piece / 120g. (yes)
Soybean milk 1 1/2 cups / 400g. (yes)
Honey 1 teaspoon / 3g. (recommended)
Cinnamon ground 1 pinch / 1g. (yes)
Acerola fruit nectar or powder 1 teaspoon / 2g. (yes)

Cooking instructions:
Cut the banana into pieces, puree them with soy milk, acerola, honey
and cinnamon with the mixing stick.

9.7 Barley and vegetable soup

Supports urination, detoxifying, promotes spleen and liver, reduces
blood pressure, strengthens immune system, prevents cancer, reduces
radiation damage, promotes digestion, helps to digest fat, harmonizes
metabolism.
Cooking time approx. 2 hours
Calories p. portion: 281
3 portions
Allergens: AGL

Quantity of ingredients:
Barley 1 cup / 120g. (yes)
Shiitake, dried 1/8 oz / 4g. (yes)
Onion (shallot) 1 piece / 20g. (yes)
Cumin (Caraway seed) 1 knife tip / 0,5g. (yes)
Sunflower oil 1 table spoon / 10g. (yes)
Water 1 cup / 250g. (yes)
Celery sticks 2 branches / 20g. (yes)
Peas, green 5/8 lbs - 8oz / 250g. (yes)
Tomato 1 piece / 50g. (yes)
Carrot 2 pieces / 150g. (yes)
French beans Handful / 30g. (yes)
Salt 1 pinch / 1g. (little)
Pepper (ground) 1 pinch / 0,5g. (yes)
Parsley 1 teaspoon / 3g. (yes)
Butter organic 1 teaspoon / 3g. (yes)

Cooking instructions:
Soak the barley in the evening for the next day. Soak the mushrooms separately at the next day. Brown onion and cumin in oil, then boil with water. Add the chopped vegetables, some salt, the barley and the shiitake mushrooms and cook everything to a thick soup. At the end, season with pepper, parsley and a little butter.

9.8 Barley mash with steamed pear

Promotes digestion, supports urination, promotes spleen, diuretic, forcing spleen, relaxes, promotes perspiration.
Cooking time approx. 25 min
Calories p. portion: 114
5 portions
Allergens: A

Quantity of ingredients:
Water 10 cups / 1200g. (yes)
Barley 1 cup / 120g. (yes)
Ginger fresh 2 slices / 2g. (yes)
Cardamom 3 capsules / 1g. (yes)
Salt 1 pinch / 1g. (little)
Pear 1 piece / 200g. (yes)
Sugar cane sugar 1/2 teaspoon / 5g. (recommended)

Cooking instructions:
Grind coarse the barley and roast it dry. Add hot water, add ginger and cardamom and let it swell to a pulp in low heat. Peel and dice the pear and boil for 10 minutes with a little water. At the end, add the stewed pear, a little butter and sweetener.

Variant: If you want to go fast, you can use barley flakes instead of shot.

9.9 Barley soup

Diuretic, forcing spleen, supports urination, stimulates liver function, antioxidativ, promotes digestion, detoxifying, reduces blood lipids, stimulates, dissolves stagnation.
Cooking time approx. 25 min
Calories p. portion: 265
2 portions
Allergens: A

Quantity of ingredients:
Barley 1 cup / 120g. (yes)
Salt 1 pinch / 1g. (little)
Ginger fresh 1/2 teaspoon / 1g. (yes)
Olive oil 1 table spoon / 10g. (yes)
Parsley 2 table spoons / 30g. (yes)
Water 1 1/2 cups / 240g. (yes)

Cooking instructions:
Roast the barley in the pan, then grind it to the ground, and boil with water, some salt and ginger to a mash. Before serving add oil and parsley.

Variant: You can add a better taste to the dish if you cook it with prepared vegetable or meat broth.

9.10 Basic recipe for a beef broth (clear)

Strengthens muscles, tendons and bones, reduces blood pressure, strengthens immune system, prevents cancer, reduces radiation damage, stimulates digestion, reduces pain, promotes digestion, diuretic. Rosemary stimulates digestion.
Cooking time approx. 4-8 hours
Calories p. portion: 114
10 portions
Allergens: 0

Quantity of ingredients:
Beef soup meat 1,1 lbs / 500g. (yes)
Beef meatbones 5/8 oz / 200g. (yes)
Vinegar (Red wine vinegar) 1 dash / 3g. (yes)
Juniper berry 8 pieces / 6g. (yes)
Rosemary 1 pinch / 1g. (yes)
Carrot 3 pieces / 210g. (yes)
Parsnip 2 pieces / 300g. (yes)
Leek 1 piece / 200g. (yes)
Ginger fresh 1/2 teaspoon / 5g. (yes)
Lovage 1 stem / 15g. (yes)
Clove 2 pieces / 2g. (yes)
Pimento 6 pieces / 12g. (yes)
Anise (Common Fennel) 2 pieces / 1g. (yes)
Salt 1 teaspoon / 5g. (little)
Water 3,3 lbs / 1300g. (yes)

Cooking instructions:
Heat water, a dash of red wine vinegar, some juniper berries, a little rosemary, bones and meat till it boils; add carrot, parsnip, leek, ginger, lovage, clove, allspice, star anise and a little salt; simmer for 4-8 hours then strain.
Refrigerate for later use.

9.11 Basic recipe for a chicken broth worming

Strengthens blood, strengthens bone marrow, reduces blood pressure, strengthens immune system, prevents cancer, reduces radiation damage, promotes sweating, dissolves stagnation, good to fight loss of appetite, flatulence.
Cooking time approx. 2-3 hours
Calories p. portion: 90
9 portions
Allergens: L

Quantity of ingredients:
Chicken meat 1/2 piece / 600g. (yes)
Carrot 2 pieces / 150g. (yes)
Leek 1 stick / 45g. (yes)
Celery root 1 piece / 500g. (yes)
Ginger fresh 2 slices / 2g. (yes)
Fenugreek (Trigonella foenum-graecum) 1 teaspoon / 2g. (yes)
Juniper berry 1 teaspoon / 3g. (yes)
Bay leaf 3 pieces / 2g. (yes)
Water 4 cup / 900g. (yes)

Cooking instructions:
Remove chicken parts from fat. Place chicken pieces in a saucepan with hot water and heat till it boils briefly, skimming any resulting foam. Add coarsely chopped vegetables and all spices and cook over medium heat for 2 to 3 hours. Strain the finished soup. Throw away vegetables and bones.
Tip: If you want to use the meat as a soup insert, take out after 45 minutes and return only the bones in the soup.
Refrigerate for later use.

9.12 Basic recipe for a duck broth

Forcing spleen, strengthens blood, supports urination, reduces blood pressure, strengthens immune system, prevents cancer, reduces radiation damage.
Cooking time approx. 2-3 hours
Calories p. portion: 61
6 portions
Allergens: L

Quantity of ingredients:
Water 2 cup / 450g. (yes)
Duck (heart) 5/8 oz / 200g. (yes)
Duck (slaughtered) 1/4 lbs - 4oz / 100g. (yes)
Carrot 2 pieces / 100g. (yes)
Celery root 1/2 piece / 600g. (yes)

Cooking instructions:
Cook duck pieces with vegetables for 2-3 hours. Sift broth through a fine sieve and refrigerate for later use.

The innards can be reused: You cut them finely and leaves them for a few minutes with fresh vegetables in the broth draw. Sprinkle with parsley before serving.

9.13 Basic recipe for a reissue soup (Congee)

Low fat content, for the drainage of the body overweight and high blood pressure.
Cooking time approx. 2-4 hours
Calories p. portion: 140
3 portions
Allergens:

Quantity of ingredients:
Rice variety any 1 cup / 120g. (yes)
Water 6 cups / 700g. (yes)

Cooking instructions:
Cook rice and water in a ratio of about 1: 6. The amount of water determines the thickness of the mash (matter of taste).
Put the rice in a saucepan with a heavy lid. It is important to simmer the rice after a short boil on the slightest flame, otherwise it burns.
Boil the rice for 2-4 hours. The longer he cooks, the more he

strengthens.
If you want to eat the dish for breakfast, you can put the rice on just before bedtime.
To be on the safe side, you should first check the behavior of your pot and cooker under observation for a similar amount of time, so that nothing burns.
Refrigerate for later use.

9.14 Basic recipe for a vegetable soup, nutritious

Reduces blood pressure, strengthens immune system, prevents cancer, forcing spleen, dissolves stagnation, promotes weight loss. Good to fight immunodeficiency, high blood pressure, depressions, diabetes, diarrhea, reduces blood lipids.
Cooking time approx. 2-3 hours
Calories p. portion: 48
5 portions
Allergens: L

Quantity of ingredients:
Olive oil 1 table spoon / 4g. (yes)
Onion white 1 piece / 60g. (yes)
Carrot 3 pieces / 200g. (yes)
Parsnip 3/8 lbs - 6oz / 150g. (yes)
Celery root 1 cup / 100g. (yes)
Ginger fresh 1/2 teaspoon / 2g. (yes)
Lemon 1/2 piece / 25g. (yes)
Juniper berry 6 pieces / 6g. (yes)
Thyme dried 1 pinch / 1g. (yes)
Lovage 1 table spoon / 3g. (yes)
Bay leaf 2 leaves / 1g. (yes)
Salt 1 pinch / 1g. (little)
Water 3 cups / 650g. (yes)

Cooking instructions:
Cut the vegetables into cubes.
Heat oil in hot pot, fry shortly onions and vegetables.
Add cold water, then add ginger, bay leaf and lemon juice.
Season with juniper, thyme and lovage. Cover for 2 - 3 hours on a low heat and simmer.
The used vegetables should be thrown away.
The basic recipe serves as a soup base and to refine vegetables, legumes or cereals.

If you want to eat vegetable soup immediately, add the desired vegetables half an hour before.
Refrigerate for later use.

9.15 Buddhist reissue soup

Little laxative. Good to fight blood circulation disorders, risk of embolism, high blood pressure, a headache, heart attack and stroke.
Cooking time approx. 2-4 hours
Calories p. portion: 280
2 portions
Allergens: G

Quantity of ingredients:
Rice variety any 1 cup / 120g. (yes)
Water 3 cups / 350g. (yes)
Butter organic 1 table spoon / 10g. (yes)
Honey 1 teaspoon / 3g. (recommended)
Cow's milk (1.5% fat) 1 cup / 120g. (yes)

Cooking instructions:
Bring the rice to boil soft in the water for 2 to 4 hours. At the end of the cooking time add some milk, honey and butter. This basic recipe can be expanded as desired (sweet, salty). The indicated quantity is sufficient for 4 days (keep in a refrigerator)

Variant: The taste can be refined with cinnamon or vanilla.

9.16 Carrot and millet bake with apple compote

Promotes spleen and liver, reduces blood pressure, strengthens immune system, prevents cancer, reduces radiation damage, calms nerves and stomach, diuretic, good to fight chronic constipation of the intestine.
Cooking time approx. 1 hour
Calories p. portion: 350
7 portions
Allergens: CGH

Quantity of ingredients:
Millet 5/8 oz / 200g. (yes)
Cow's milk (whole milk 3.5% fat) 2 cups / 450g. (recommended)
Lemon peel 1/2 piece / 2g. (yes)
Sugar brown 2 table spoons / 20g. (recommended)
Carrot 7/8 lbs / 400g. (yes)
Ginger fresh 2 teaspoons / 6g. (yes)
Acerola fruit nectar or powder 1 teaspoon / 2g. (yes)
Almond puree 1/8 lbs - 2oz / 50g. (yes)
Chicken egg 4 pieces / 240g. (yes)
Yogurt (natural, 1.5% fat) 3/8 lbs - 6oz / 150g. (yes)
Butter organic 1 teaspoon / 4g. (yes)
Apple (sour) 4 pieces / 600g. (recommended)
Water 1 cup / 300g. (yes)
Clove 2 pieces / 1g. (yes)
Sugar brown 1 table spoon / 10g. (recommended)

Cooking instructions:
Preheat the oven to 100°C/212°F (with circulating air 8o°C/176°F, gas level 2).
Heat the milk with the millet till it boils, add lemon zest and sugar. Cover and simmer for 5 minutes, then simmer in a preheated oven for 20 minutes. Switch oven to medium heat.
Peel apples and cut into small pieces, boil with water, cloves and sugar for about 5 minutes.
Mix the millet in a bowl with the grated carrots, finely chopped ginger and acerola.
Mix the almond paste (or butter) with the hand mixer. Add egg yolk and stir everything to a smooth cream. Mix in sour cream. Add millet and carrots.
Beat the egg whites very stiff and lift them under the millet pulp. Brush out a baking dish with butter. Add the millet and bake in a preheated oven for 45 minutes on a low heat.
Serve with the apple compote.

9.17 Carrot and rice gruel soup

Stops diarrhea, good to fight fever, strengthens immune system, reduces blood pressure.
Cooking time approx. 10 min
Calories p. portion: 101
1 portions
Allergens:

Quantity of ingredients:
Basic recipe for a rice soup (Congee) 1 cup / 120g. (yes)
Carrot 2 pieces / 100g. (yes)
Salt 1 teaspoon / 4g. (little)

Cooking instructions:
Peel and grate carrots. Heat the rice soup (according to the basic recipe) till it boils and add the grated carrots and salt. Cook for 10 minutes.

9.18 Carrot rice with chicken

Promotes spleen and liver, reduces blood pressure, strengthens immune system. Strengthens blood, strengthens bone marrow. Strengthens spleen and stomach, strengthens the muscles. Provides Vitamin C.
Cooking time approx. 30 min
Calories p. portion: 116
2 portions
Allergens: G

Quantity of ingredients:
Carrot (Early Carrot) 3/8 lbs - 6oz / 150g. (yes)
Chicken meat 1/8 lbs - 2oz / 40g. (yes)
Butter organic 2 teaspoons / 6g. (yes)
Water 1 cup / 250g. (yes)
Rice round grain 1 oz / 30g. (yes)
Orange juice 2 table spoons / 20g. (recommended)

Cooking instructions:
Clean, wash and peel the carrots and grate. Cut the chicken breast into small cubes, sauté in 1 teaspoon of butter, add the carrots and rice. Add the water and heat till it boils. Cook over low heat for about 20 minutes. Put the carrot rice on a dish, add the remaining butter and orange juice.

9.19 Carrot soup

Promotes spleen and liver, reduces blood pressure, strengthens immune system, prevents cancer, reduces radiation damage, improves blood circulation, improves medication effect, increase Appetite, stimulates liver function.
Cooking time approx. 30 min
Calories p. portion: 210
2 portions
Allergens: O

Quantity of ingredients:
Carrot 1,1 lbs / 500g. (yes)
Pepper (ground) 1 pinch / 0,5g. (yes)
Nutmeg 1 pinch / 1g. (yes)
Salt 1 pinch / 1g. (little)
White wine 1/2 cup / 125g. (little)
Orange juice Alternatively for wine / g. (recommended)
Parsley 2 table spoons / 10g. (yes)
Peppers powder 1 pinch / 1g. (yes)
Thyme dried Alternative to rose paprika / g. (yes)
Pine nuts 1 table spoon / 15g. (yes)
Sunflower seeds Alternatively to pine nuts / g. (yes)

Cooking instructions:
Place peeled large cut carrot pieces in hot water; cook and then puree; season with ground pepper, a little nutmeg, a pinch of salt; add a dash of white wine and simmer for a few minutes or season with orange juice; Add parsley as desired; stir in some rose paprika or fresh thyme; sprinkle with roasted pine nuts or sunflower seeds before serving.

9.20 Carrots with potato foam

Promotes spleen and liver, reduces blood pressure, strengthens immune system. Improves digestion, regenerates skin, supports urination, lowers cholesterol, promotes the production of stool and urine, strengthens blood, strengthens nerves.
Cooking time approx. 30 min
Calories p. portion: 316
1 portions
Allergens: G

Quantity of ingredients:
Carrot (Early Carrot) 3/8 lbs - 6oz / 150g. (yes)
Pork meat 1/8 lbs - 2oz / 40g. (yes)
Potato (mealy) 1/4 lbs - 4oz / 100g. (yes)
Butter organic 1 table spoon / 10g. (yes)
Honey 1/2 teaspoon / 2g. (recommended)
Anise (Common Fennel) 1 pinch / 0,2g. (yes)
Water 2 table spoons / 20g. (yes)

Cooking instructions:
Clean the carrots, wash thoroughly, peel thinly and cut into thin slices.
Cut the meat into strips.
Wash the potatoes, cook in a small saucepan with little water in about 15 minutes.
Melt half of the butter in a saucepan, fry the carrots and the meat in it. If necessary, add 2-3 tablespoons of water, put the lid on and cook everything over low heat in about 15 minutes.
Add the honey, the anise and the remaining butter and remove the pot from the heat.
Peel the potatoes and press directly onto the plate with the potato press. Distribute the honey carrots over it.

9.21 Chicken soup with egg yolk and parsley

Strengthens blood, strengthens bone marrow, reduces blood pressure, strengthens immune system. Parsley stimulates liver function, harmonizes liver and spleen, strengthens eyesight, detoxifying.
Cooking time approx. 10 min
Calories p. portion: 118
2 portions
Allergens: CL

Quantity of ingredients:
Basic recipe for a chicken soup (warming) 2 cup / 500g. (yes)
Chicken yolk 1 piece / 10g. (yes)
Parsley 1 table spoon / 10g. (yes)

Cooking instructions:
Cook the chicken broth according to the basic recipe.
Heat broth and bubble the egg yolk. Sprinkle the chopped parsley over it and let it rest for about 2 minutes. Drink in small sips.

9.22 Corn coffee with cardamom

Diuretic, forcing spleen, supports urination, relaxes, reduces fat.
Cooking time approx. 5 min
Calories p. portion: 3
1 portions
Allergens:

Quantity of ingredients:
Cereal coffee 1 table spoon / 15g. (yes)
Cardamom 2 cores / 1g. (yes)
Water 1 cup / 120g. (yes)

Cooking instructions:
Boil water, coffee, sugar and cardamom. Let it set for one min before drinking.

9.23 Cranberry yogurt mix

Good to fight acute or chronic constipation of the intestine, oral mucosal inflammation, diarrhea, flatulence, throat irritation.
Cooking time approx. 5 min
Calories p. portion: 57
2 portions
Allergens: GO

Quantity of ingredients:
Yogurt (natural, 1.5% fat) 1/4 lbs - 4oz / 125g. (yes)
Cranberry jam 2 table spoons / 20g. (yes)
Mineral water 1 cup / 250g. (yes)

Cooking instructions:
Mix yoghurt, cranberry jam and mineral water until frothy.

9.24 Curdcheesedumplings on strawberry pulp

Strawberry forcing spleen and stomach, strengthens blood. Chicken egg calms nerves and stomach.
Cooking time approx. 30 min
Calories p. portion: 553
5 portions
Allergens: ACG

Quantity of ingredients:
Curd cheese 20% 1,1 lbs / 500g. (yes)
Spelled semolina 3/8 lbs - 6oz / 150g. (yes)
Butter organic 1/8 lbs - 2oz / 40g. (yes)
Chicken egg 2 pieces / 120g. (yes)
Sugar - icing sugar 2 table spoons / 20g. (recommended)
Salt 1 pinch / 1g. (little)
Breadcrumbs (wheat bread, bread roll) 2 table spoons / 25g. (yes)
Butter organic 1/4 lbs - 4oz / 100g. (yes)
Strawberries 1,1 lbs / 500g. (yes)
Sugar - icing sugar 2 table spoons / 25g. (recommended)

Cooking instructions:
Curdcheese, grit, butter, eggs, powdered sugar and salt to a smooth dough. Keep the dough 15 mins in the refrigerator to settle down. Then shape small dumplings with a diameter of approx 4cm and boil them for about 10 minutes in slightly boiling salt water. Heat butter in a pan and roast the breadcrumbs golden brown. Roll the dumplings carefully into the crumbs.
Serve the dumplings with the strawberry.

9.25 Fennel-Rice Soup

Forcing spleen, relieves constipation, stimulates nerves, detoxifying, reduces inflammation, improves blood circulation.
Cooking time approx. 15-20 min
Calories p. portion: 156
2 portions
Allergens: EG

Quantity of ingredients:
Basic recipe for a rice soup (Congee) 1 cup / 300g. (yes)
Fennel 1/2 piece / 150g. (yes)
Butter organic 1 table spoon / 15g. (yes)
Soy sauce 1 dash / 3g. (yes)

Cooking instructions:
Cook the fennel softly in the rice soup according to the basic recipe. Before serving, add a piece of butter and some soy sauce.

9.26 Fresh full-grain porridge

Regulates gastrointestinal function. Reduces Inflammation, relieves pain, detoxifying, bactericide.
Cooking time approx. 15 min
Calories p. portion: 336
1 portions
Allergens: AG

Quantity of ingredients:
Spelled wholemeal flour 1 oz / 25g. (yes)
Cow's milk (whole milk 3.5% fat) 3/4 cup - 6 oz / 200g. (recommended)
Honey 1 teaspoon / 3g. (recommended)
Banana 1 piece / 120g. (yes)

Cooking instructions:
Grind the cereal grains into a flour mill. You may also be able to use a coffee grinder, but then grind twice. Stir the flour with the milk in a saucepan and bring it to boil over medium heat. Cook the porridge on low heat for 4-5 minutes while stirring. Then add the honey. Crush the banana with a fork and pull it under the porridge.

9.27 Frozen pineapple juice

Pineapple reduce inflammation, supports urination, cleans the skin.
Cooking time approx. 1 1/2 hours
Calories p. portion: 29
1 portions
Allergens:

Quantity of ingredients:
Pineapple 1/8 lbs - 2oz / 50g. (yes)

Cooking instructions:
Juice pineapple yourself or freeze the organic pineapple juice in small portions and if necessary suck.

9.28 Frozen salami tea

Sage dries out, good to fight yeast infections
Cooking time approx. 1 1/2 hours
Calories p. portion: 16
2 portions
Allergens:

Quantity of ingredients:
Sage 1 table spoon / 10g. (yes)
Water 2 cup / 500g. (yes)

Cooking instructions:
Add sage to hot water.
10 min. to let go.
30 min. to let cool down.
Freeze in small portions.
Suck as needed.

9.29 Honey milk

Calming, good to fight insomnia. Little laxative. Relieves pain, detoxifying, bactericide.
Cooking time approx. 5 min
Calories p. portion: 88
1 portions
Allergens: G

Quantity of ingredients:
Cow's milk (whole milk 3.5% fat) 1 cup / 120g. (recommended)
Honey 1 teaspoon / 4g. (recommended)

Cooking instructions:
Heat the milk gently and add the honey. Drink in small sips.

9.30 Lentils and rice stew

Promotes spleen and kidney, is very nutritious, reduces blood pressure, strengthens immune system. Good to fight blood circulation disorders, thromboses, risk of embolism, high blood pressure, a headache. Strengthens heart and kidney, diuretic, calms the stomach, promotes digestion.
Cooking time approx. 25 min
Calories p. portion: 232
3 portions
Allergens: LNO

Quantity of ingredients:
Lentils 1/4 lbs - 4oz / 100g. (yes)
Water 5 cups / 500g. (yes)
Rice variety any 1 cup / 120g. (yes)
Sesame oil 1 table spoon / 10g. (yes)
Carrot 2 pieces / 150g. (yes)
Celery sticks 2 rods / 20g. (yes)
Cumin (Caraway seed) 1 pinch / 0,2g. (yes)
Salt 1 pinch / 0,5g. (little)
Vinegar (Apple vinegar) 1 dash / 2g. (yes)
Parsley 2 table spoons / 18g. (yes)

Cooking instructions:
Soak the dry lentils the day before.
Heat sesame oil in a hot pot; cut carrot and celery into small pieces and
sauté; add rice, a pinch of cumin and lentils and heat till it boils.
If the lenses are soft, add salt; season with a little vinegar and garnish
with parsley.

Variant: In summer you can omit the cumin and add fresh green peas,
Chinese cabbage or celery.

9.31 Mango banana yoghurt drink ice cold

Good to fight loss of appetite, oral mucosa inflammation. Regulates
gastrointestinal function, chronic constipation. Prevents cancer.
Diuretic, forcing spleen.
Cooking time approx. 5 min
Calories p. portion: 121
2 portions
Allergens: G

Quantity of ingredients:
Mango juice 1/2 cup / 100g. (recommended)
Yogurt (natural, 1.5% fat) 1/4 lbs - 4oz / 100g. (yes)
Mineral water 1/2 cup / 100g. (yes)
Banana 1/2 piece / 150g. (yes)
Acerola fruit nectar or powder 1 teaspoon / 2g. (yes)

Cooking instructions:
Mix all the ingredients and 2-3 ice cubes in a blender.

9.32 Millet mash with steamed pears

Calms stomach, strengthens tendons and bones, supports urination.
Promotes digestion, supports urination. Diuretic, building up, eye-
enhancing, detoxifying, nerve-strengthening.
Cooking time approx. 25 min
Calories p. portion: 235
3 portions
Allergens:

Quantity of ingredients:
Millet 1 cup / 100g. (yes)
Water 1 1/2 cups / 220g. (yes)
Cardamom 1 pinch / 0,5g. (yes)
Pear 1-2 pcs. Biological / 250g. (yes)
Salt 1 pinch / 0,2g. (little)
Grape juice red 1 cup / 250g. (recommended)
Cinnamon ground 1 pinch / 0,2g. (yes)
Clove 2 pieces / 0,4g. (yes)
Lemon juice 1 table spoon / 8g. (yes)

Cooking instructions:
Roast millet while stirring until it smells well.
Cool the pot briefly.
Add 2 cups of hot water, the cardamom and a pinch of salt.
On low flame, covered, for 20 min. simmer.
Quarter the pears, remove the core, peel on request, add about ¼ liter
of red grape juice, cinnamon stick, cloves, lemon juice and a pinch of
salt) and simmer gently covered for a few minutes.

9.33 Millet with pears

Refreshing and nourishing, promotes digestion, supports urination,
good to fight cough, promotes perspiration, reduces blood lipids,
stimulates, dissolves stagnation, forces liver, strengthens the muscles,
lowers cholesterol, antiparasitic.
Cooking time approx. 35 min
Calories p. portion: 213
5 portions
Allergens: G

Quantity of ingredients:
Millet 1 cup / 120g. (yes)
Water 1 1/2 cups / 200g. (yes)
Grape juice red 1 1/2 cups / 240g. (recommended)
Pear 4 pieces / 600g. (yes)
Ginger fresh 1/2 teaspoon / 2g. (yes)
Salt 1 pinch / 1g. (little)
Acerola fruit nectar or powder 1 teaspoon / 2g. (yes)
Cocoa 1 pinch / 1g. (yes)
Sunflower seeds 2 table spoons / 4g. (yes)
Barley malt 1/2 teaspoon / 2g. (yes)
Cream, sweet 30% 2 teaspoons / 20g. (recommended)

Cooking instructions:
Simmer the millet for 5 min and let it swell for another 30 min.
Then: In a hot pot, heat some grape juice; add chopped pears, very little
grated ginger, a pinch of salt, acerola, a pinch of cocoa and sauté
briefly; add the boiled millet, sunflower seeds, some barley malt to
taste, 1 tsp cream per serving or a little butter.

9.34 Noodle soup

Protects the digestive system. Detoxifying, affects anorexia, reduces
blood pressure, strengthens immune system, strengthens the muscles,
tendons and bones. stimulates liver function, detoxifying.
Cooking time approx. 1 1/2 hours
Calories p. portion: 237
8 portions
Allergens: ACEGL

Quantity of ingredients:
Beef soup meat 3/4 lbs / 300g. (yes)
Water 4 cup / 900g. (yes)
Bay leaf 1 piece / 1g. (yes)
Carrot 3/4 lbs / 300g. (yes)
Celery sticks 1 bunch / 200g. (yes)
Cauliflower 3/4 lbs / 300g. (yes)
Parsley 1 Bunch / 100g. (yes)
Noodles (wheat) with egg 3/4 lbs / 300g. (yes)
Butter organic 1 table spoon / 10g. (yes)
Salt 1 teaspoon / 2g. (little)
Soy sauce 1 table spoon / 8g. (yes)
Tomato paste 1 table spoon / 10g. (yes)

Cooking instructions:
Simmer the meat and bay leaf in the water over low heat for about 30 minutes.
Peel and slice the carrots.
From the celery plant separate the lower end and the leaves. Wash the stems, peel off the tough threads and cut
the stems into slices about 1 cm thick.
Wash the Brussels sprouts, clean them and cut the roses from below crosswise.
Wash and chop the parsley.

Add the Brussels sprouts and carrot slices to the soup and cook for about 30 minutes.

After about 10 minutes, add the celery and green leaves and the pasta. Finally, remove the bay leaf and celery green.

(For the baby, remove about 200-250 g of carrots, celery and noodles with broth, squeeze about 35 g of meat finely and add to the baby soup, stir in the butter and 1 teaspoon of chopped parsley.)

Season the remaining soup with the salt, the soy sauce, the tomato paste and the remaining parsley. Lift out the meat. Remove fat and bones and dice the meat. Serve in the soup.

9.35 Parsley cream sauce

Reduces blood pressure, strengthens immune system, forcing spleen, dissolves stagnation, improves digestion, lowers cholesterol. Stimulates liver function, detoxifying.
Cooking time approx. 25 min
Calories p. portion: 118
2 portions
Allergens: GL

Quantity of ingredients:
Basic recipe for a vegetable soup (nutritious) 3/4 lbs / 300g. (yes)
Potato 1/4 lbs - 4oz / 100g. (yes)
Parsley 1 Bunch / 15g. (yes)
Nutmeg 1 pinch / 0,5g. (yes)

Coriander 1/2 teaspoon / 1g. (yes)
Sour cream 15% fat 1/8 lbs - 2oz / 50g. (recommended)
Fennel seeds ground 1/2 teaspoon / 1g. (yes)
Ginger powder 1 pinch / 0,5g. (yes)

Cooking instructions:
Broth the vegetable soup according to the basic recipe with peeled, diced potatoes, half of the finely chopped parsley and nutmeg. Cover and simmer until the potatoes are tender.

Using the blender, puree the vegetable broth, potatoes, remaining freshly chopped parsley, fennel, ginger and sour cream into a smooth sauce.

9.36 Pear compote

Promotes digestion, supports urination.
Cooking time approx. 20 min
Calories p. portion: 100
3 portions
Allergens:

Quantity of ingredients:
Water 1 1/2 cups / 240g. (yes)
Pear 4 / 500g. (yes)

Cooking instructions:
Halve organic pears. Cores and skin can be used. Pear in the pot and add water. Simmer for up to 20 minutes until pears are tender.

9.37 Pear with candy sugar and sticky rice

Promotes digestion, supports urination. Strengthens spleen and stomach.
Cooking time approx. 50 min
Calories p. portion: 217
4 portions
Allergens: GH

Quantity of ingredients:
Pear 2 pieces / 300g. (yes)
Sugar candy white 1 teaspoon / 4g. (recommended)
Lemon 1/2 piece / 10g. (yes)
Water 2 cup / 500g. (yes)

Acerola fruit nectar or powder 1 teaspoon / 2g. (yes)
Rice sticky 1 cup / 120g. (yes)
Water 3 cups / 300g. (yes)
Almond puree 2 table spoons / 20g. (yes)
Cream (30% fat) 2 table spoons / 20g. (recommended)
Maple syrup 1-2 table spoon / 15g. (recommended)
Cinnamon ground 1 pinch / 1g. (yes)

Cooking instructions:
Simmer halved unpeeled organic pear (with seeds) with sugar candy
and half of the lemon covered approx. 20min.
After cooling, add acerola.
Cook the rice with water (1: 3) about 45min. Cover and cook on the
lowest heat.
Form the rice into small balls. Arrange the pears with the juice with the
rice balls. Decorate the pears with almond purée and whipped cream. If
you like it sweeter, sweeten with maple syrup. Sprinkle with cinnamon.

9.38 Porridge

Strengthens immune system. Little laxative.
Cooking time approx. 15 min
Calories p. portion: 208
2 portions
Allergens: AG

Quantity of ingredients:
Oat flakes (whole grain) 8 table spoons / 60g. (yes)
Water 1/2 cup / 125g. (yes)
Cow's milk (whole milk 3.5% fat) 1/2 cup / 125g. (recommended)
Salt 1 pinch / 0,3g. (little)
Cream, sweet 30% 2 table spoons / 20g. (recommended)
Sugar cane sugar 1 table spoon / 8g. (recommended)

Cooking instructions:
Heat water and milk and a pinch of salt till it boils. Sprinkle in 4
tablespoons of coarse rolled oats and cook to a pulp, add 4 tablespoons
of fine oatmeal and let it swell. Arrange in a preheated bowl and top
with cream.

9.39 Potato cream with herbs and fresh cheese

Good to fight loss of appetite, constipation, bloating and nausea. Improves digestion, supports urination, prevents cancer, forcing spleen, dissolves stagnation, relaxing and reassuring.
Cooking time approx. 25 min
Calories p. portion: 217
2 portions
Allergens: G

Quantity of ingredients:
Potato (mealy) 5/8 lbs - 8oz / 250g. (yes)
Fresh cheese 3 oz / 80g. (yes)
Yogurt (natural, 1.5% fat) 2 table spoons / 45g. (yes)
Chives 1/2 bunch / 50g. (yes)
Basil (fresh) 1 teaspoon / 4g. (yes)
Parsley 1 teaspoon / 4g. (yes)
Dill 1/2 teaspoon / 2g. (yes)
Salt 1 pinch / 1g. (little)
Black caraway 1 pinch / 0,5g. (yes)
Pepper (ground) 1 pinch / 0,5g. (yes)

Cooking instructions:
Softly steam the potatoes in the pan, peel them and press through the potato press.
Mix cream cheese, yoghurt and herbs under the potatoes, season with salt, crushed black cumin and pepper.

9.40 Potatoes with curd cheese sauce

Improves digestion, supports urination, lowers cholesterol. Good to fight weakness, belching, diabetes, acute or chronic obstruction of the bowel, skin problems. Good to fight Bloating, cramping in gastrointestinal complaints.
Cooking time approx. 45 min
Calories p. portion: 414
6 portions
Allergens: G

Quantity of ingredients:
Potato 2,2 lbs / 1000g. (yes)
Curd cheese 20% 1,1 lbs / 500g. (yes)
Cream, sweet 30% 5/8 oz / 200g. (recommended)
Edam cheese 3 oz / 80g. (yes)

Dill 1 Bunch / 100g. (yes)
Corn germ oil 1 teaspoon / 3g. (yes)
Pepper (ground) 1 pinch / 0,2g. (yes)
Salt 1/2 teaspoon / 1g. (little)
Sunflower seeds 1/8 lbs - 2oz / 40g. (yes)

Cooking instructions:
Wash the potatoes and cook in plenty of water for about 20 minutes.
Stir the creamy cheese with the cream and cottage cheese. Wash the
sprouts, finely chop. Stir in with the chopped dill. (For the baby, mix 150
g. of pot with the oil.) Mix the rest with pepper, salt and the sunflower
seeds. Peel the potatoes, arrange (for the baby 200 g.) with the pot.

9.41 Puréed banana

Eat 2 times a day, regulates gastrointestinal function
Cooking time approx. 7 min
Calories p. portion: 144
1 portions
Allergens:

Quantity of ingredients:
Banana 1 piece / 150g. (yes)

Cooking instructions:
Mix the banana with the fork or purée with a blender. Leave to brown for
at least 5 minutes.

9.42 Rice noodle soup with shiitake mushrooms

Very light and powerful. Strengthens the immune system.
Cooking time approx. 20 min
Calories p. portion: 66
2 portions
Allergens: L

Quantity of ingredients:
Rice noodles 2 handful / 20g. (yes)
Shiitake, dried 4-6 pieces / 5g. (yes)
Basic recipe for a vegetable soup (nutritious) 1 1/2 cups / 240g. (yes)
Chinese cabbage 1 cup / 60g. (yes)
Lovage 1 teaspoon / 3g. (yes)
Miso 2 table spoons / 18g. (yes)

Cooking instructions:
Soak rice noodles and shiitake mushrooms separately in cold water.
Heat the vegetable broth and add the soaked shiitake mushrooms cut
into strips and simmer gently. Cut Chinese cabbage into noodles, add
lovage green and rice noodles and let it steep for a while. Before
serving, stir in Miso dissolved in a little cooled water.

Recommendation: Suitable at the beginning of each meal, also for
breakfast

9.43 Rice soup with grated carrots and fresh herbs

Diuretic, warming the body from the inside, expands blood vessels,
strengthens the muscles, regulates internal organs functions, reduces
blood pressure, strengthens immune system, prevents cancer, reduces
radiation damage. Promotes digestion.
Cooking time approx. 5 min
Calories p. portion: 131
4 portions
Allergens: EG

Quantity of ingredients:
Rice wild (nature rice) 1 cup / 100g. (yes)
Water 6 cups / 700g. (yes)
Carrot 1 piece / 100g. (yes)
Soy sauce 1 dash / 2g. (yes)
Butter organic 1 teaspoon / 3g. (yes)
Ground 1 pinch / 0,3g. (yes)
Curcuma 1 pinch / 0,2g. (yes)
Herbs various 1 teaspoon (chopped) / 3g. (yes)

Cooking instructions:
In a portion of rice congee according to basic recipe, softly cook a
grated carrot, add butter and soy sauce.
Sprinkle with fresh herbs.

Spices and herbs: black cumin, turmeric, cardamom, parsley, sage,
thyme, basil, rosemary.

Winter: parsnip, celery, onion, leek, pumpkin
Summer: tomatoes, zucchini, spring onion, radishes, arugula.

9.44 Rice with parsnips

Rich in vitamins, minerals potassium and zinc. Good to fight blood circulation disorders, thrombose, risk of embolism, high blood pressure, a headache, heart attack and stroke, yeast infections.
Cooking time approx. 45 min
Calories p. portion: 206
3 portions
Allergens:

Quantity of ingredients:
Rice variety any 1 cup / 120g. (yes)
Water 1 1/2 cups / 200g. (yes)
Salt 1 pinch / 1g. (little)
Parsnip 3-4 pieces / 450g. (yes)
Olive oil 1 table spoon / 10g. (yes)
Sage 1 teaspoon / 3g. (yes)

Cooking instructions:
Peel the parsnips and cut into slices. Fry for a short time in oil. Add the rice and fry again for a short time. Add the water and cook it at least 30 min. Sprinkle with fresh chopped sage.

9.45 Rice with stewed vegetables

Reduces blood pressure, strengthens immune system, prevents cancer, reduces radiation damage, extremely low fat content, good to fight blood circulation disorders, thrombose, risk of embolism, a headache, heart attack and stroke. Is diuretic.
Cooking time approx. 20 min
Calories p. portion: 166
2 portions
Allergens: L

Quantity of ingredients:
Rice variety any 1/2 cup / 60g. (yes)
Water 3 cups / 300g. (yes)
Lemon peel 1 piece / 3g. (yes)
Water 1/2 cup / 0g. (yes)
Carrot 2 pieces / 180g. (yes)
Celery sticks 1/2 piece / 5g. (yes)
Champignon 1/2 cup / 50g. (yes)
Cress 2 table spoons / 20g. (yes)
Linseed oil 1 dash / 3g. (yes)

Cooking instructions:
Cook rice according to basic recipe with a piece of lemon peel.
Steam chopped carrots, celery and mushrooms until soft.
Then sprinkle with cress. Then add a dash of high quality cold oil.

9.46 Semolina dumpling soup

Reduces blood pressure, strengthens immune system, prevents cancer, reduces radiation damage, dissolves stagnation, promotes weight loss. Good to fight immunodeficiency, loss of appetite, flatulence, high blood pressure, depressions, diabetes, diarrhea.
Cooking time approx. 1 hour
Calories p. portion: 287
3 portions
Allergens: ACGLO

Quantity of ingredients:
Butter organic 1/8 lbs - 2oz / 40g. (yes)
Chicken egg 1 piece / 65g. (yes)
Salt 1 pinch / 1g. (little)
Pepper (ground) 1 pinch / 0,5g. (yes)
Nutmeg 1 pinch / 1g. (yes)
Wheat semolina 3 oz / 80g. (yes)
Basic recipe for a beef soup (warming) 2 cup / 500g. (yes)
Parsley 1 table spoon / 10g. (yes)
Chives 1 table spoon / 10g. (yes)

Cooking instructions:
Knead the ingredients for the dumplings to a firm dough and allow to swell for 30 minutes. Heat the broth (basic recipe for a beef broth warming). Then cut out with a spoon dumplings, place in the prepared broth and let stand for 20 minutes. Before serving, chop parsley and sprinkle with thinly sliced chives.

9.47 Semolina dumpling + mascarpone and strawberry sauce

Relieves pain and inflammation, little laxative. Protects the digestive system. Detoxifying, affects anorexia, good to fight flatulence, inflammatory bowel disease, obesity, gout, stomach ulcers, stomach cramps, rheumatism, heartburn, twelffinger intestinal ulcers.
Cooking time approx. 25 min
Calories p. portion: 331
3 portions
Allergens: AG

Quantity of ingredients:
Cow's milk (1.5% fat) 1 1/2 cups / 400g. (yes)
Wheat semolina 0,2 lbs / 70g. (yes)
Cinnamon ground 1 pinch / 0,5g. (yes)
Lemon peel 1 pinch / 1g. (yes)
Honey 1 teaspoon / 3g. (recommended)
Vanilla pod 1 pinch / 0,5g. (yes)
Mascarpone cheese 3 oz / 80g. (recommended)
Strawberries 1,1 lbs / 500g. (yes)
Honey 1 table spoon / 10g. (recommended)

Cooking instructions:
In a small saucepan, heat the milk till it boil while stirring. Stir in semolina, cinnamon and lemon peel and cook 6 minutes stirring until thick, firm paste.

Mix the semolina, honey, vanilla and mascarpone into a smooth mixture with the hand mixer. Allow the mass to cool in the refrigerator.

For the sauce, puree strawberries with honey in a blender.
Spread a few spoons of fruit sauce on a large plate.
With 2 tablespoons, cut off dumplings from the semolina mass (to prevent sticking, rinse in cold water again and again). Put the dumplings on the fruit souce.

It looks especially nice when the dessert is still garnished with a few berries and herbal leaves.

9.48 Semolina porridge with banana

Regulates gastrointestinal function, reduces inflammation, antiallergic, good to fight blood circulation disorders.
Cooking time approx. 15 min
Calories p. portion: 307
1 portions
Allergens: AG

Quantity of ingredients:
Cow's milk (whole milk 3.5% fat) 3/4 cup - 6 oz / 200g. (recommended)
Spelled semolina 2 table spoons / 30g. (yes)
Butter organic 1 teaspoon / 4g. (yes)
Banana 1/2 piece / 50g. (yes)

Cooking instructions:
Heat the half of the milk in a small pot. Add the semolina and boil it shortly in the milk. Let it swell at low heat for 3 minutes with constant stirring. Remove the pot from the heat, add the remaining milk with the snow bean and place the mush in a small bowl. Add the butter and the battered banana. For adults, a pinch of cinnamon can be spread over it.

9.49 Semolina soup with vegetables

Reduces blood pressure, strengthens immune system, prevents cancer, forcing spleen, dissolves stagnation, promotes weight loss. Good to fight immunodeficiency, loss of appetite, flatulence, high blood pressure, depressions, diabetes, diarrhea, rheumatism, heartburn, twelffinger intestinal ulcers.
Cooking time approx. 20 min
Calories p. portion: 105
3 portions
Allergens: AGL

Quantity of ingredients:
Basic recipe for a vegetable soup (nutritious) 2 cup / 500g. (yes)
Wheat semolina 2 table spoons / 20g. (yes)
Lovage 1/2 teaspoon / 2g. (yes)
Basil (fresh) 1/2 teaspoon / 1g. (yes)
Nutmeg 1 pinch / 0,1g. (yes)
Carrot 1/4 lbs - 4oz / 100g. (yes)
Celery root 1/8 lbs - 2oz / 50g. (yes)
Cream, sweet 30% 2 table spoons / 30g. (recommended)
Parsley 1 table spoon / 10g. (yes)

Cooking instructions:
Roast wheat grits without fat in a pan. Roast the chopped carrots and celery briefly. Add the vegetable soup (Basic recipe for a vegetable soup). Season with lovage, nutmeg and let it 10 min. simmer. Stir in the cream before serving and garnish with parsley.

9.50 Soup with egg yolk

Strengthens muscles, tendons and bones, reduces blood pressure, strengthens immune system.
Cooking time approx. 5 min
Calories p. portion: 173
1 portions
Allergens: CO

Quantity of ingredients:
Basic recipe for a beef soup (warming) 1 cup / 250g. (yes)
Chicken yolk 1 piece / 25g. (yes)

Cooking instructions:
Warm the beef soup according to the basic recipe for a beef broth, warm it up and jell the yolk.

9.51 Strawberry yoghurt and almond puree mix

Relieves pain and inflammation in rheumatism. Good to fight acute or chronic constipation of the intestine. Little laxative. Relieves pain, detoxifying, bactericide.
Cooking time approx. 5 min
Calories p. portion: 134
3 portions
Allergens: GH

Quantity of ingredients:
Yogurt (natural, 1.5% fat) 5/8 oz / 200g. (yes)
Strawberries 1,5 lbs / 700g. (yes)
Honey 1 teaspoon / 3g. (recommended)
Acerola fruit nectar or powder 1 teaspoon / 2g. (yes)
Almond puree 2 teaspoons / 6g. (yes)

Cooking instructions:
Puree yoghurt, strawberries, acerola, honey and almond paste in a blender.

9.52 Supplementary nutrition

Protein-rich drink with very high energy density. Optimized protein content balances nitrogen losses and promotes protein anabolism.
Cooking time approx. 5 min
Calories p. portion: 1045
1 portions
Allergens:

Quantity of ingredients:
Supplementary nutrition 1 package / 250g. (recommended)

Cooking instructions:
Use only as directed by the physician or therapist.

9.53 Sweet rice with apples

Stops diarrhea, promotes digestion, appetizing, stops coughing, supports urination, many antioxidants. Little laxative.
Cooking time approx. 25 min
Calories p. portion: 156
4 portions
Allergens: H

Quantity of ingredients:
Rice sweet 1 cup / 100g. (yes)
Water 6 cups / 600g. (yes)
Apple juice (natural cloudy) 1 cup / 120g. (recommended)
Apple (sweet) 2 pieces / 300g. (recommended)
Apricot 2 pieces / 200g. (recommended)
Cinnamon ground 1 pinch / 0,3g. (yes)
Cardamom 1 pinch / 0,2g. (yes)
Ginger powder 1 knife tip / 0,3g. (yes)
Salt 1 pinch / 0,3g. (little)
Lemon 1/2 cut into pieces / 10g. (yes)
Cocoa 1 pinch / 0,5g. (yes)
Almond puree 2 table spoons / 20g. (yes)
Barley malt 1 table spoon / 10g. (yes)
Hazelnuts 2 table spoons / 20g. (yes)

Cooking instructions:
Cook sweet rice in hot water.
Then: heat apple juice in a hot pot; chopped sweet apples, apricots or other sweet fruit (neutral or warm), cinnamon, cardamom, ginger, a

pinch of salt, grated lemon peel, a little cocoa and simmer for a few minutes.
Stir in the boiled sweet rice, a little almond paste, some barley malt and heat; sprinkle with roasted nuts.

9.54 Tea from anise

Anise (wild fennel) promotes digestion, forcing spleen and stomach.
Cooking time approx. 15 min
Calories p. portion: 3
4 portions
Allergens:

Quantity of ingredients:
Anise (Common Fennel) 1 teaspoon / 3g. (yes)
Water 2 cup / 500g. (yes)

Cooking instructions:
Heat the water till it boils and put it aside. Add anise.
10 min. to let go.
Pour through a tea strainer. Sweet to taste with honey.

In order to achieve a salutary effect, you should drink 2 cups of anise tea per day.

9.55 Tea from blue mallow

Good to fight stomach pain, gastritis.
Cooking time approx. 10 min
Calories p. portion: 0
2 portions
Allergens:

Quantity of ingredients:
Blue mallow tee 2 table spoons / 14g. (yes)
Water 2 cup / 500g. (yes)

Cooking instructions:
Heat the water till it boils and put it aside. Add cheesecloth tea and 10 min. to let go. Sweet to taste with honey.
Strain when pouring.

9.56 Tea from chamomile

Good to fight flatulence, nausea, intestinal cramps, diarrhea, inflammation of the oral mucosa, influenza infections, stomach and intestinal mucosa infections, badly healing wounds, nausea, colds, skin rashes, inflammation in the genital and anal area.
Cooking time approx. 10 min
Calories p. portion: 0
1 portions
Allergens:

Quantity of ingredients:
Chamomile 1 teaspoon / 3g. (yes)
Water 1 cup / 120g. (yes)

Cooking instructions:
Heat the water till it boils and put it aside. Chamomile flowers added and 10 min. to let go.

9.57 Tea from fennel

Harmonizes stomach, less bloating.
Cooking time approx. 10 min
Calories p. portion: 0
4 portions
Allergens:

Quantity of ingredients:
Fennel tea 2 table spoons / 20g. (yes)
Water 2 cup / 500g. (yes)

Cooking instructions:
Heat the water till it boils and put it aside. Add fennel tea and 10 min. to let go. Sweet to taste with honey. Strain when pouring.

9.58 Tea from mallow

Relieves irritation cough, soothes mucous membranes in mouth, throat, stomach and intestines, inhibits inflammation, easily contracting (astringent).
Cooking time approx. 10 min
Calories p. portion: 0
4 portions
Allergens:

Quantity of ingredients:
Mallow (Malva sylvestris) blossom tea 2 teabags / 4g. (yes)
Water 2 cup / 500g. (yes)

Cooking instructions:
Heat the water till it boils and put it aside. Add mallow tee and 10 min.
to let go. Sweet to taste with honey. Strain when pouring.

9.59 Tea from sage

Sage dries out, good to fight yeast infections.
Cooking time approx. 15 min
Calories p. portion: 4
4 portions
Allergens:

Quantity of ingredients:
Sage 2 teaspoons / 6g. (yes)
Water 2 cup / 500g. (yes)

Cooking instructions:
Heat the water till it boils and put it aside. Add sage and 10 min. to let
go. Strain. Sweet to taste with honey.

9.60 Tender fennel vegetables

Relieves constipation, stimulates nerves, reduces inflammation,
improves blood circulation, regenerates skin, supports urination.
Promotes digestion.
Cooking time approx. 25 min
Calories p. portion: 70
2 portions
Allergens: G

Quantity of ingredients:
Potato 1 piece / 50g. (yes)
Fennel 1/4 lbs - 4oz / 100g. (yes)
Water 2 table spoons / 20g. (yes)
Butter organic 1 table spoon / 10g. (yes)

Cooking instructions:
Wash the potato and peel with a peeler. Cut into cubes of about 2 cm.
Wash the fennel, remove stained, dark spots and cut the tuber. Heat till

it boils with 2 tablespoons of water in a small saucepan. Cook on low heat for about 15 minutes. Fish out the caraway seeds. Puree the vegetables with the blender and stir in the butter.
Fennel and caraway soothe the stomach and prevent bloating. In addition, fennel contains a lot of vitamin C and folic acid. An ideal meal for sick children.

9.61 Vanilla pudding

Helps to fight constipation.
Cooking time approx. 10 min
Calories p. portion: 254
2 portions
Allergens: G

Quantity of ingredients:
Cow's milk (whole milk 3.5% fat) 2 cups / 500g. (recommended)
Pudding powder vanilla 1 package / 37g. (yes)
Sugar white 1 table spoon / 12g. (recommended)

Cooking instructions:
Give 3-5 tablespoons of milk into a cup, bring the rest in a pot to boil. Pour the powdered pudding into the cup and stir until free of lumpy. As soon as the milk boils, add the mixture and simmer under low heat for about 3 minutes.
Divide into prepared bowls.

9.62 Vegetable potato and meat mash

Strengthens immune system, reduces inflammation, improves digestion, strengthens spleen and stomach, strengthens the muscles, tendons and bones, antiparasitic.
Cooking time approx. 30 min
Calories p. portion: 127
2 portions
Allergens:

Quantity of ingredients:
Potato 1/4 lbs - 4oz / 100g. (yes)
Carrot (Early Carrot) 5/8 oz / 200g. (yes)
Beef meat (calf) 1/8 lbs - 2oz / 40g. (yes)
Apricots juice 6 table spoons / 60g. (recommended)
Rapeseed oil 1 table spoon / 6g. (yes)

Cooking instructions:
Remove the flesh, skin, tendons and grease, wash under cool water and cut into small pieces and boil in a little water. After about 15-20 minutes, remove and puree. Wash the vegetables and potatoes, peel and cut into not too small pieces. Cook gently with a little water over a low heat for 10-20 minutes. Use the blender to chop the vegetables. Mix everything, add butter or oil and fruit juice and puree again.
Alternately use other meats such as chicken, lamb or turkey. Also change vegetables with zucchini, kohlrabi, fennel, pumpkin, parsnips and broccoli.
Also change the fruit juices. This can produce a variety of flavors.

9.63 Vegetable rice

Forcing spleen, dissolves stagnation, promotes weight loss. Good to fight immunodeficiency, loss of appetite, flatulence, high blood pressure, strengthens kidney and bladder. Diuretic, warming the body from the inside, regulates internal organs functions.
Cooking time approx. 30 min
Calories p. portion: 304
3 portions
Allergens: L

Quantity of ingredients:
Broccoli 1/8 lbs - 2oz / 50g. (yes)
Carrot 1/8 lbs - 2oz / 50g. (yes)
Kohlrabi 1/8 lbs - 2oz / 50g. (yes)
Cauliflower 1 oz / 30g. (yes)
Peas 1/2 oz / 20g. (yes)
Margarine 1 teaspoon / 4g. (yes)
Rice (whole grain) 5/8 oz / 200g. (yes)
Basic recipe for a vegetable soup (nutritious) 7/8 lbs / 400g. (yes)
Parsley 1/2 oz / 20g. (yes)
Pepper (ground) 1 pinch / 0,2g. (yes)

Cooking instructions:
Cut the broccoli, carrots and kohlrabi into small cubes, divide the cauliflower into small florets. Heat the margarine in a pan or saucepan, sauté the vegetables. Then add the rice, top up with the vegetable stock and leave to soak for 15-20 minutes.
In the meantime finely chop the parsley. After cooking, season the rice with freshly ground pepper and parsley.

9.64 Vegetable semolina soup

Diuretic, harmonizes the stomach and intestines, conducts bowel winds, reduces blood pressure, lowers cholesterol, detoxifying, good to fight loss of appetite, flatulence, inflammatory bowel disease, heartburn, twelffinger intestinal ulcers. Stimulates digestion, reduces pain.
Cooking time approx. 20 min
Calories p. portion: 199
3 portions
Allergens: AEGL

Quantity of ingredients:
Basic recipe for a vegetable soup (nutritious) 2 cup / 500g. (yes)
Potato 1 piece / 80g. (yes)
Parsnip 1 piece / 180g. (yes)
Carrot 1 piece / 120g. (yes)
Celery root 3/8 lbs - 6oz / 150g. (yes)
Kohlrabi 1/2 piece / 200g. (yes)
Beans (green, fresh) 1/4 lbs / 100g. (yes)
Wheat semolina 2 table spoons / 24g. (yes)
Lovage 1/2 teaspoon / 2g. (yes)
Butter organic 1 table spoon / 20g. (yes)
Soy sauce 1 teaspoon / 3g. (yes)

Cooking instructions:
Worm the prepared vegetable soup; cook the vegetables in the soup softly. Spread some wheatgrass and let it swell. At the end, add lovage-green and a little butter and taste with soy sauce.

9.65 Yellow lentil soup

Strengthens heart and kidney, diuretic, promotes spleen, calms the stomach, promotes digestion, strengthens immune system, prevents cancer, reduces radiation damage, stimulates liver function, antioxidativ.
Cooking time approx. 20 min
Calories p. portion: 155
7 portions
Allergens: A

Quantity of ingredients:
Lentils yellow 1 lbs / 500g. (yes)
Carrot 2 pieces / 150g. (yes)
Kohlrabi 1 piece / 300g. (yes)

Onion white 1 piece / 50g. (yes)
Parsley 1/2 bunch / 100g. (yes)
Turmeric (yellow root) 1 pinch / 1g. (yes)
Cardamom 1 pinch / 1g. (yes)
Salt 1 pinch / 1g. (little)
Olive oil 1 table spoon / 10g. (yes)
Water 4 cup / 1000g. (yes)
Lemon juice 1/2 piece / 15g. (yes)
White bread (wheat bread) 7 slices / 140g. (yes)

Cooking instructions:
Wash lenses well in a colander. Heat oil in a pot. Add finely chopped onion, sliced carrots, diced kohlrabi and spices, sauté and salt. Add the lentils and cover with water and simmer for 20 minutes. Add water as needed and season with salt. Sprinkle with fresh parsley or fresh green cilantro and drizzle with lemon juice.
Here you can also use red lenses. (same cooking time).
Serve with white bread.

9.66 Zucchini semolina cream soup

Good to fight loss of appetite, reduces blood pressure, promotes weight loss. Good to fight loss of appetite, flatulence, inflammatory bowel disease, rheumatism, heartburn.
Cooking time approx. 25 min
Calories p. portion: 146
4 portions
Allergens: AGL

Quantity of ingredients:
Butter organic 1/2 oz / 20g. (yes)
Wheat semolina 2 table spoons / 20g. (yes)
Parsley 1 Bunch / 100g. (yes)
Basic recipe for a vegetable soup (nutritious) 3 1/2 cups / 800g. (yes)
Lovage 1/2 teaspoon / 2g. (yes)
Nutmeg 1 pinch / 0,5g. (yes)
Anise (Common Fennel) 1 pinch / 0,5g. (yes)
Zucchini 7/8 lbs / 400g. (yes)
Ginger fresh 1/2 teaspoon / 1g. (yes)
Créme fraiche cheese 2 table spoons / 20g. (yes)
Lemon peel 1/4 piece / 2g. (yes)
Salt 1 pinch / 1g. (little)
Pepper (ground) 1 pinch / 0,5g. (yes)

Cooking instructions:

Melt the butter in a saucepan, add the semolina and fry briefly while stirring. Add half of the chopped parsley, sauté for a short time, pour vegetable broth according to the basic recipe, season with chopped lovage, nutmeg and anise. Cook the soup without lid lightly for 10 minutes. Add the finely chopped zucchini and the small piece of lemon zest, cook gently for 5 minutes until the zucchini are tender. Remove the lemon peel.

Using the blender, finely puree the soup with the crème fraiche and the remaining parsley.

10 Effects of food

10.1 Use ingredients: recommendable

Acai powder
Apple (sour)
Apple (sweet)
Apple juice (natural cloudy)
Apple puree
Apricot
Apricots juice
Berry juice
Bitter Herb liqueur
Bitter Lemon
Blueberry juice
Cherry compote
Cherry juice
Clarified butter
Clementines
Compote (fruits of the season)
Cow's milk (whole milk 3.5% fat)
Cream (30% fat)
Cream 10% coffee cream
Cream sour 30%
Cream, sweet 30%
Fox nut, gorgon nut, makhana
Fructose (glucose)
Fruit mix juice

Grape juice red
Grape juice white
Hibiscus
Honey
Kudzu
Lily bulbs
Mango juice
Maple syrup
Mascarpone cheese
Orange juice
Pear juice
Sour cream 15% fat
Sour milk
Sugar - icing sugar
Sugar brown
Sugar candy white
Sugar cane sugar
Sugar molasses
Sugar palm sugar
Sugar white
Supplementary nutrition
Walnuts
Walnuts roasted

10.2 Use ingredients: yes

Acerola fruit nectar or powder
Adzuki beans
Agar agar (kelp)
Agave nectar
Agrimony
Almond
Almond marzipan
Almond milk
Almond puree
Aloe juice
Amaranth
Amaranth Pops
Anchovy / Sardine
Angelica root
Anise (Common Fennel)
Apricot dried
Apricot jam
Apricot nectar
Apricots
Arrowroot
Artichoke
Asparagus (green or white)

Aubergine
Avocado
Baking powder
Balm
Bamboo shoots
Banana
Banana (cooking banana)
Banchatee (green tea)
barberry
Barley
Barley flour
Barley grass powder
Barley grouts
Barley malt
Barley not peeled
Basic recipe for a beef soup
Basic recipe for a beef soup (warming)
Basic recipe for a chicken soup
(warming)
Basic recipe for a duck soup
Basic recipe for a fish soup
Basic recipe for a rice soup (Congee)

Basic recipe for a vegetable soup
(nutritious)
Basil
Basil (fresh)
Batavia
Bay leaf
Bean oil
Beans (green, fresh)
Bearberry leaf
Beef bone marrow
Beef fillet
Beef heart
Beef heart (calf)
Beef kidney
Beef liver
Beef lungs (calf)
Beef meat
Beef meat (calf)
Beef meatbones
Beef Oxtail pieces
Beef soup meat
Beef stomach
Beer (alcohol-free)
Beer (alcohol-reduced)
Berries of the season
Bitter orange peel
Black beans
Black caraway
Black fungus mushroom
Black tea
Blackberry dried (unripe fruit)
Blackberry jam
Blackberry leaves
Blackberry´s
Black-eyed peas
Blackthorn (Sloe)
Blue mallow tee
Blueberry
Blueberry dried
Blueberry jam
Bocksdorn fruits (Fructus Lycii, Goji,
goji berry dried
Boletus mushroom
Borage
Borage oil
Boxhorn clover seeds
Brazil nuts
Bread roll
Bread with carob kernel flour
Breadcrumbs (wheat bread, bread roll)
Brie cheese
Broad beans (thick beans)
Broccoli
Brussels sprouts

Buckbean
Buckwheat
Buckwheat (roasted) Kasha
Buckwheat whole grain
Bulgur (cereals)
Burdock root tea
Bush beans
Butter (half fat)
Butter beans white
Butter organic
Buttermilk
Calamari
Camembert
Cantaloupe
Capers in olive oil
Carambola (Star fruit)
Cardamom
Carob flour, St. john's bread
Carp
Carrot
Carrot (Early Carrot)
Carrot juice without sugar
Cashews
Cauliflower
Caviar
Celery root
Celery sticks
Cereal coffee
Chamomile
Chamomile tea
Champignon
Channa-Dal
Chanterelle
Chard
Chenpi (chinese tangerine bowl)
Cherry
Cherry (sour)
Chervil
Chervil dried
Chestnut puree
Chestnuts
Chicken Blood
Chicken egg
Chicken egg white
Chicken heart
Chicken liver
Chicken meat
Chicken stomach
Chicken yolk
Chickpeas
Chickweed
Chicory
Chili (pod or ground)
Chinese cabbage

Chinese pearl barley
Chives
Chlorella (fresh water)
Chocolate
Chocolate (Diabetic)
Chrysanthemum blossom tea
Cinnamon ground
Cinnamon sticks
Clementine
Clove
Cocoa
Coconut fat
Coconut flakes
Coconut grated
Coconut meat
Coconut milk
Cod
Codfish
Coffee
Coix (seeds) YiYi Ren
Cola drink
Cooking oil
Coriander
Coriander (fresh)
Corn
Corn (fast polenta)
Corn (roasted)
Corn flour
Corn germ oil
Corn Grease (Polenta)
Corn silk tea
Corn starch
Cottage cheese
Couscous
Cow's milk (1.5% fat)
Crab
Cranberries
Cranberry
Cranberry
Cranberry jam
Cranberry juice
Cream sour 10%
Cream sour 20%
Creamer
Créme fraiche cheese
Cress
Crispbread
Crucian
Cucumber
Cucumber (bitter)
Cucumber (spicy cucumber)
Cumin (Caraway seed)
Curcuma
Curd cheese 20%

Curd cheese 40%
Currant (black)
Currant (red)
Currant (white)
Currant jam (black)
Currant jam (red)
Currant juice (black)
Currants (black)
Currants (red)
Curry
Curry paste red
Daisy
Dandelion (young plants)
Dandelion juice
Dandelionroots tea
Dashi
Dates dried
Dates red
Deer meat
Deer meat
Deer's Bones
Deer's kidneys
Dill
Duck (heart)
Duck (slaughtered)
Ducks egg
Dulse (seaweed)
Dyer's broom herb
Edam cheese
Eel
Elderberries
Elderberry blossom tee
Emmental cheese
Endive salad
Evening primrose oil
Fennel
Fennel seeds ground
Fennel tea
Fenugreek (Trigonella foenum-graecum)
Feta cheese
Feta cheese
Fig
Fig dried
Fish innards
Fish pieces mixed (fresh water)
Fish remains
Fish sauce
Flounder
Flower pollen
French beans
Fresh cheese
Fresh cheese from soya
Fresh cheese with herbs

Freshwater crab
Freshwater fish
Fruit tea
Gail plum
Galangal
Garam Masala powder
Garlic
Gelatin white
Gelee Royal
Gentian root
Gentian root tea
Ginger fresh
Ginger oil
Ginger powder
Ginkgo fruit
Ginseng
Ginseng root
Goat
Goat and sheep's blood
Goat and sheep's brain
Goat and sheep's liver
Goat and sheep's milk
Goat and sheep's stomach
Goat cheese
Goose
Goose blood
Goose egg
Goose fat
Goose parts
Gooseberry
Gorgonzola
Gouda cheese
Gourd
Grapefruit (Pomelo)
Grapefruit dried peel
Grapefruit juice
Grapes red
Grapes white
Grapeseed oil
Grass carp
Green spelt
Green tea
Greengage
Ground
Ground caraway
Guava
Halibut (Flatfish)
Hawthorn
Hazelnuts
Herbal tea mix
Herbs bitter
Herbs of Provence
Herbs various
Herbs wild

Herring
Hibiscus tea
Hijiki
Hokkaido pumpkin
Hop
Horehound leaves
Horse meat
Hyssop
Iceberg lettuce
Jasmine blossoms tee
Jellyfish
Juniper berry
Kaki plum
Kalmus
Kefir
Kidney beans (red)
King Solomon's-seal
Kiwi
Kohlrabi
Kombu seaweed (Saccharina japonica)
Kukicha tea
Kumquats
Ladyfingers
Lamb bones
Lamb kidneys
Lamb liver
Lamb meat
Lamb shoulder
Lamb's lettuce
Lamb's lettuce
Lavender blossoms
Leaf salads (bitter)
Leek
Lemon
Lemon Balm (dried)
Lemon Balm (fresh)
Lemon juice
Lemon peel
Lemongrass
Lentils
Lentils black
Lentils red
Lentils yellow
Lettuce
Licorice root tea
Lima beans
Lime
Lime blossom tea
Linseed
Linseed (crushed)
Linseed oil
Liver smoothing tea
Lobster
Longane

Loquate / Japanese medlar
Lotus roots
Lotus seeds
Lovage
Lovage seeds
Luo Han Guo fruit
Lychee
Lychee in Preserved
Lye roll
Mackerel
Mallow (Malva sylvestris) blossom tea
Malt
Mango
Manioc flour
Mare's milk
Margarine
Margarine (diet)
Marjoram
Mayonnaise 50%
Mayonnaise 80%
Mediterranean fish (cod, plaice,
haddock, sea eel, mackerel)
Medlar
Millet
Millet flakes
Mineral water
Mirabelle plum
Miso
Miso black (fermented)
Miso paste (soy bean paste)
Mixed Pickles
Mold cheese
Morel (black, dried)
Morel, dried
Mozzarella
Mu Erh Mushroom
Muesli
Mulberry fruit
Mulled Wine Spice
Mullet
Multi-grain bread (gray bread)
Mung bean
Mung bean sprouting
Mussels
Mustard
Mustard Dijon
Mustard medium hot
Mustard seeds
Mustard sweet
Mutton
Mutton
Nasturtium (nose-twister or nose-
tweaker)
Nectarine

Nettles
Noodles (wheat) with egg
Noodles (wheat, lasagne) with egg
Noodles (wheat, ribbon noodles) with
egg
Noodles (wheat, spaghetti) with egg
Noodles (whole grain) with egg
Nori, purple seaweed, red algae
Nutmeg
Oat
Oat flakes (whole grain)
Oat flakes roasted
Oat flour
Oat fusion (baby food)
Oat meal
Oat milk
Octopus
Octopus
Okra
Olive oil
Olives
Olives green
Onion (shallot)
Onion (spring onion)
Onion read
Onion white
Orange
Orange blossom
Orange dried peel
Orange grated peel
Orange jam
Orange peel
Oregano dried
Oregano fresh
Oyster mushroom
Oyster shell powder
Oysters
Palm oil
Papaya
Parmesan
Parsley
Parsley root
Parsnip
Passion blossoms tea
Passion fruit
Peaches
Peaches (canned)
Peanut (roasted)
Peanut butter
Peanut oil
Peanuts
Pear
Pearl barley
Pearl barley

Peas
Peas, green
Pepper (ground)
Pepper Cayenne
Pepper powder (hot)
Pepper white (ground)
Peppercorns
Peppermint
Peppermint tea
Pepperoni
Pepperoni, red, pitted, halved
Pepperoni, yellow, pitted, halved
Peppers
Peppers (rose peppers)
Peppers (sweet)
Peppers powder
Perch
Pheasant
Pickle
Pig blood
Pigeon
Pigeon egg
Pimento
Pine nuts
Pineapple
Pineapple (from a can)
Pineapple juice without sugar
Pinto beans speckled
Pistachios
Plaice
Plum
Plum dried
Plums
Pomegranate
Poppy
Pork Bacon
Pork brain
Pork fat (lard)
Pork ham
Pork ham cooked
Pork ham smoked
Pork heart
Pork kidneys
Pork knuckle
Pork Lard
Pork liver
Pork lung
Pork marrow bones
Pork meat
Pork skin
Pork stomach
Pork/beef sausage (smoked)
Pork's intestine
Potato

Potato (mealy)
Potato flour
Prickly pear
Processed cheese 12%
processed cheese 30%
Psyllium seed
Pudding powder vanilla
Puff pastry
Pumpernickel (dark bread)
Pumpkin
Pumpkin seed oil
Pumpkin seeds
Quail
Quail egg
Quince
Quinoa
Rabbit
Rabbit (wild)
Rabbit liver
Rabbit meat
Radicchio
Radish
Radish (white, green, purple-red)
Radish black
Radish horseradish
Radish leaves
Raisins
Rapeseed oil
Raspberry
Raspberry dried (immature)
Raspberry jam
Raspberry leaf tea
Red beet
Red berry (without sugar)
Red cabbage
Red wine
Reishi mushroom
Rhubarb
Ribworttea
Rice (fragrance)
Rice (Gaoliang / Sorghum)
Rice (whole grain)
Rice Basmati
Rice black
Rice flour
Rice long grain rice
Rice malt
Rice mash
Rice noodles
Rice red
Rice round grain
Rice starch
Rice sticky
Rice sweet

Rice variety any
Rice wild (nature rice)
Romaine lettuce / lettuce salad
Rose blossom tea
Rose hip
Rose hip tea
Rose leaf tea
Rosefish
Rosemary
Rucola
Rusk
Rye
Rye flour
Rye wholemeal bread
Safflower (Dyer's thistle / Hong Hua)
Saffron
Sage
Sago (cereals)
Sake
Salmon
Salsify
Sauerkraut (cutted cabbage fermented)
Savory
Savoy cabbage / kale
Sea buckthorn
Sea cucumber
Seacrab
Sesame oil
Sesame oil roasted
Sesame paste (Tahini)
Sesame, black
Sesame, white
Shark
Sheep's milk
Sheep's milk yoghurt
Shiitake, dried
Shrimp
Shrimps
Skim milk powder
Slug
Sorrel
Sour cherries
Sour milk cheese 20%
Sourdough
Soy flour
Soy noodles
Soy sauce
Soy Tofu
Soy Tofu smoked
Soya Cuisine (soy cream)
Soybean milk
Soybean oil
Soybeans
Soybeans, black

Soybeans, blacks, fermented
Soybeans, yellow
Spelled (Dark) bread
Spelled flakes
Spelled grain
Spelled semolina
Spelled wholemeal flour
Spinach
Spiny lobsters
Spurdog (spiny dogfish, Schillerlocken)
St. Benedict's thistle, blessed thistle,
holy thistle, spotted thistle
Star anise
Stevia (candyleaf, sweetleaf)
Strawberries
Strawberry jam
Strawberry Juice
Sugar fructose - fruit sugar
Sugar glucose - grapes sugar
Sugar Milk Sugar
Sugar substitute (sweetener)
Sunflower oil
Sunflower seeds
Sweet potato
Tabasco
Tangerine
Tarragon (Estragon)
Tea mixture uric acid lowering
Thistle oil
Thyme
Thyme dried
Toast bread (whole grain)
Tomato
Tomato dried
Tomato juice
Tomato paste
Tomato puree
Tonic Water
Topinambur
Trout
Trout (smoked)
Truffle
Tsampa (roasted barley flour)
Tuna
Turkey breast meat
Turkey ham
Turmeric (yellow root)
Turnip
Turnips
Umeboshi paste
Umeboshi plums (Japanese apricots)
Valerian
Vanilla
Vanilla pod

Vanilla powder
Vanilla sugar natural
Vegetable juice
Vinegar (Apple vinegar)
Vinegar (Red wine vinegar)
Vinegar Aceto Balsamico
Vinegar Aceto Balsamico white
Wakame
Walnut oil
Water
Water hot
Watermelon
Wax gourd
Wheat
Wheat bran
Wheat bulgur
Wheat flakes
Wheat flatbread/pita bread
Wheat flour
Wheat flour whole grain
Wheat germ oil
Wheat semolina
Wheat semolina for children
Wheat/Rye/Gray-black bread with yeast
Wheatgrass juice
Wheatgrass powder
Whey

White beans
White bread (baguette)
White bread (pretzel sticks)
White bread (roll)
White bread (wheat bread)
White breadcrumbs
White cabbage
White dumpling bread (wheat bread cut into chunks)
Whitefish
Whole grain bread
Wholemeal flour
Wild boar meat
Wild garlic (garlic spinach)
Wild herbs
Wild strawberries
Wormwood herb
Yam root, yam root tuber
Yarrow
Yarrow tea
Yeast
Yew nut
Yoghurt vanilla
Yogi tea
Yogurt (natural, 1.5% fat)
Yogurt (natural, 3.5% fat)
Zucchini

10.3 Use ingredients: little

Beer (Pils)
Beer (Top-fermented German dark beer)
Bitter liqueur
Brown ale
Campari
Cola drink (low calorie)
Eel smoked
Fernet Branca (herbal bitter liqueur)
Ginseng liqueur
Honey wine (Met)
Lychee liqueur

Martini
Pork sausage (Bratwurst)
Prosecco
Rum
Salt
Salt (herbal)
Sherry (whine)
Spirit
Wheat beer
White wine
Wormwood

10.4 Do not use contra-acting foods

-

11 Herbs and their effects

11.1 Basil (fresh)

It has a beneficial effect on flatulence and nausea, relaxing and soothing. Good to fight emphysema, bronchitis, whooping cough, high blood pressure, headache, mouth odor, warts, hiccup, gout, migraine.

11.2 Dill

The medicinal and spice herb has an antispasmodic effect and stimulates gastric juice production. Good to fight flatulence. Antispasmodic for gastrointestinal discomfort.

11.3 Chamomile

Antispasmodic and anti-inflammatory for digestive disorders, soothes the nerves and promotes good sleep. Applied externally, it heals wounds in the mouth-throat area and the skin. Strengthens eyesight.

11.4 Coriander

The essential oils are appetizing, digestive, cramping and soothing in stomach and intestinal disorders.

11.5 Herbs various

Appetizing, lots of trace elements and vitamins

11.6 Cress

Diuretic, supports urination. Good to fight dry mouth, inner agitation, sore throat, diabetes, kidney stones, gastrointestinal complaints, lung problems, menstrual cramps or cancer.

11.7 Chives

Bactericide, prevents cancer, strengthens gastric juice production, promotes digestion and blood circulation, promotes growth, triggers stagnation.

11.8 Lovage

Stimulates digestion, reduces pain. Extracts of the root are used to flush out urinary tract infections and prevent kidney gravel.

11.9 Parsley

Stimulates liver function, detoxifies. Forces urinating. Relieves flatulence. Digestive and menstrual stimulating, birth-accelerating, memory-enhancing, blood-purifying, skin-smoothing.

11.10 Rosemary

Promotes digestion, relieves bloating, strengthens lung, spleen and kidney. Affects the circulation and nerves. Appetizing. Baths help to fight circulatory disorders as well as with gout and rheumatism.

11.11 Sage

Good to fight yeast infections. The leaves have a digestive effect and are used in greasy foods. Antiperspirant effect. Helps to relieve coughing attacks. Dries out (TCM).

11.12 Black caraway

Detoxifying, immunoregulatory. In addition, the oil should stimulate the formation of bone marrow cells and generally protect body cells from viruses.

11.13 Thyme dried

Disinfecting. It stimulates the blood circulation, increases the appetite and helps to digest fat meat better. Strengthens lungs and spleen (TCM).xx

12 Basics of Nutrition

The basic principles of nutrition described herein are general recommendations. They are not aimed at a specific form of therapy. Recommendations concerning a therapy have priority.

12.1 Nutrition

Regular meals in a relaxed atmosphere. A warm breakfast is considered a good start into the day.

The main meals ought to be taken for lunch – supper in the early evening. Pay attention to feeling hungry or sated: don't eat too much nor remain hungry is the rule

Prepare the meals freshly from natural, regional products. Frozen, heat-conserved, industrially prepared or foodstuffs cooked in the microwave oven are rejected.

Choice of foodstuffs according to the season: more cooling food in summer, more warming food in winter.

Eat cooked food at least twice a day. Food and drinks ought to be lukewarm, never ice-cold or hot.

Raw vegetables, briefly cooked vegetables, freshly squeezed juices and mineral water are not recommended. Milk and dairy products are only included in the diet if they don't cause problems.

Don't use therapeutic recipes over a longer period without consulting your doctor or therapist.

Varied food

Enjoy the diversity of foodstuffs. Characteristics of a balanced nutrition are variety, suitable combination and a balanced quantity of rich and low energy foodstuffs (on one hand avoiding undersupply with essential nutrients and on the other hand to take to many undesirable substances).

A lot of Cereal Products - and Potatoes

Bread, pasta, rice, cereal flakes (best wholemeal) as well as potatoes contain almost no fat, but many vitamins, mineral nutrients, trace elements, roughage and secondary plant substances. These foodstuffs ought to be taken with low-fat side dishes.

Vegetables and Fruit – „Take Five" every day …

5 portions of vegetables and fruit a day, as fresh as possible, briefly cooked, or maybe one portion as a juice – ideal as a side dish to every meal as well as snack between meals: Thus a lot of vitamins, mineral nutrients as well as roughage and secondary plant substances

Daily milk and dairy products
Milk and Dairy Products every Day, once or twice per Week Fish; meat, sausages as well as eggs moderately. These foodstuffs contain valuable nutrients like calcium in the milk, iodine selenium and omega-3 fat acids in saltwater fish. Meat is favorable due to its high content of disposable iron and the vitamins B1, B6 and B12. Quantities of 300 – 600 g meat and sausage per week are sufficient. Prefer low-fat products, especially in meat- and dairy products.

Low-fat and fatty Foodstuffs
Fat supplies us with essential fat acids and fatty foodstuffs contain also fat-soluble vitamins. Fat is high in energy; therefore much fat in the food may cause overweight, possibly also cancer. Too many saturated fat acids may further a tendency for cardio-vascular diseases in the long term. Prefer vegetable oils and fats (e.g. rapeseed-, olive-, soya-oils and solid fats produced therefrom). Beware of invisible fat in meat- and dairy products, pastry and sweets as well as in fast-food and convenience foods. 70 – 90 g fat per day is sufficient.

Moderately Sugar and Salt
Take sugar and foods/drinks containing various kinds of sugar (e.g. glucose syrup) only occasionally. Use herbs and spices as well as a little salt creatively. Prefer salt containing iodine.

Plenty of Liquids
Water is absolutely essential. Drink 1-2 l liquids every day. Prefer water (with or without gas) and other low-calorie drinks. Alcoholic drinks should not be taken.

Tasty Dishes, carefully cooked
Cook the meals with as low temperatures and as short as possible, using little water and fat – this preserves the original taste, keeps the nutrients intact and prevents the production of harmful compounds.

Take time and enjoy the food
Take your Time and enjoy your Food
Eating consciously helps to eat right. The eye enjoys food, too. It's fun, invites to enjoy varied dishes and stimulates the feeling of satiety.

Watch your Weight and stay in Motion
A balanced diet and a lot of exercise and sport (30 – 60 min/day) are a healthy combination. The right weight furthers well-being and health. Thermals, directional effectiveness, digestive power

There are various criteria for judging the effectiveness of herbs and foodstuffs.
The use of certain herbs and ingredients is based on observations of the effects on the body which these foodstuffs, herbs and spices show after having eaten them. The medical science has developed following system: Every ingredient or herb has a directional effectiveness. Furthermore, there are herbs which have a special effect on certain organs.
The basic condition for a healthy metabolism is to obtain sufficient energy from food and that the digestive process doesn't use too much energy. An easily digestible meal makes content and sated, doesn't cause flatulence and fatigue after the meal. The perfect spices increase the healthiness of our meals. Very often, just small doses of herbs and spices will suffice. They are not used to make us sated, but to help our digestive organs to digest the food.

12.2 Recipes

The recipes list the ingredients to be used and the cooking instructions show how the dish is prepared. The list of ingredients shows the concerned quantities as well as the relevance for the therapy. If you find „less than mentioned", try to comply or find an alternative from the „list of recommended foodstuffs". Mostly it shall result just in a small change of taste when you simply avoid this ingredient.
Mild cooking methods: boiling, stewing, poaching, steaming
Strong cooking methods: barbecuing, roasting, frying, smoking
Balanced cooking methods: deep-frying, baking brick
Deep-freezing and warming in the microwave oven should be avoided (denaturalization).

12.3 Foodstuffs

Foodstuffs have an effect on body and soul like medicinal herbs, only a very much milder one. Dietary advice is mainly based on regional foodstuffs. The knowledge about the effects of each foodstuff and the knowledge, when which foodstuff shall be used, is based on the orthodoschool of medicine. Use ecologic-organic products, if possible. As everything should be cooked for a long time due to a better digestability and very rarely eaten raw, the food agrees with everyone.
The classification of the foodstuffs according to their effect on the body is the basis in order to achieve a harmonious status of health.

Dietary advisors do not recommend certain foodstuffs for everyone. The individual diet is tailor-made for the individual constitution.

Buy only fresh and ripe fruit and vegetables. You ought to leave unripe fruit and vegetables and such with brown spots and wilted leaves behind in the market. In this case take deep-frozen goods (never ready-to-serve dishes!). Fruit and vegetables are deep-frozen immediately after harvesting and often contain more vitamins and minerals than the goods from the vegetable shelf. Whereas conserved or tinned goods contain very much less biological substances. Also, salt, sugar and others are mostly added to the latter. Never leave the foodstuffs in the water after washing them to avoid that many vital substances get drowned. Clean salads, fruit and vegetables immediately before serving.

Please make sure of the hygienic processing of foodstuffs. Clean your salads, fruit and vegetables carefully. When cooking with meat, prepare all ingredients first and then process the meat products. Clean the worktop and tools very carefully. Wooden surfaces ought to be treated with a mild disinfectant regularly in order to reduce germination.

Store fruit and vegetables separately, if possible. Harvested fruit and vegetables are still alive and emit e.g. ethylene gas, which makes other products ripen and age faster. Keep meat and fish in the closed packaging or store them in the fridge in closed containers.

12.4 Herbs

There are some basic rules for storing medicinal herbs. On principle, herbs must be protected from direct sunlight, humidity and heat.

Containers for the storage of herbs may be glasses, ceramic jars and even plastic containers. However, plastic is a rather unsuitable material and should only be a short-term solution. In case of glass containers, use a dark material.

Medicinal herbs cannot be kept for any long period. The shelf life of herbs is limited. However, it can be prolonged with suitable storage. The place should be dark, rather cool and absolutely dry. A wooden medicine cabinet, placed not directly next to a source of heat, would be ideal. Never buy large quantities of herbs so as not to have to throw them away. Label the container with the name of the herb and the date of harvesting or processing.

13 Other dietic-books

The following syndromes of dietetics, TCM or for a therapy supplement for cancer are available.

Dietetics

E001. Nutrition of the infant - baby food
E002. Nutrition during lactation
E003. Nutrition in old age
E004. Nutrition of children and adolescents
E005. Nutrition of athletes
E006. Light weight
E007. Pregnancy
E008. Full food

Protein and electrolyte - kidneys
E009. (hemodialysis) dialysis treatment
E010. Acute renal failure
E011. Chronic renal insufficiency
E012. Nephrotic syndrome
E013. Kidney stones (nephrolithiasis)

Gastrointestinal tract - pancreas
E014. Acute pancreatitis (inflammation of the pancreas)
E015. Chronic pancreatitis (inflammation of the pancreas)

Gastrointestinal tract - small intestine and large intestine
E016. Acute obstipation (constipation)
E017. Chronic obstipation (constipation)
E018. Colon irritabile
E019. Diverticulitis
E020. Acquired lactose intolerance (lactose malabsorption)
E021. Fructose malabsorption
E022. Glutensensitive enteropathy (celiac disease)
E023. Colectomy
E024. Short Bowel Syndrome

Gastrointestinal tract - liver, gallbladder, bile ducts
E025. Acute and chronic hepatitis (inflammation of the liver)
E026. Cholelithiasis (bile stones)
E027. fatty liver
E028. cirrhosis

Gastrointestinal tract - Stomach and duodenal intestine
E029. Acute gastritis
E030. Chronic gastritis
E031. Stomach bleeding
E032. Ulcus ventriculi and duodenal ulcer
E033. Condition after gastric surgery

Gastrointestinal tract - oral cavity and esophagus
E034. Stomatitis
E035. Esophageal carcinoma (esophageal cancer)
E036. Refluosophagitis (heartburn)

Special diseases
E037. Phenylketonuria (PKU)
E038. Rheumatic joint diseases

Metabolism
E039. Obesity (overweight)
E040. Diabetes mellitus
E041. Eating disorders (underweight)

Fat metabolism
E042. Hypercholesterolaemia (increased cholesterol level)
E043. Hepatic Encephalopathy

Heart and circulation
E044. Arteriosclerosis (arterial calcification)
E045. Heart insufficiency
E046. Hypertension
E047. Hyperuricaemia and gout

Changed nutrient requirements
E048. In case of fever
E049. For malignant diseases
E050. After burns
E051. Radiation and chemotherapy

CANCER
E100. Pancreatic cancer
E101. Bladder cancer
E102. Blood cancer (leukemia)
E103. Breast cancer
E104. Colorectal cancer
E105. Gastric cancer
E106. Kidney cancer
E107. Esophageal cancer

TCM
E200. Bladder - moisture heat in the bladder
E201. Bladder - moisture and cold in the bladder
E202. Bladder - emptiness and cold in the bladder
E203. Large intestine - external cold affects the large intestine
E204. Large intestine - moisture heat in the large intestine
E205. Large intestine - heat blocks the intestine II acute
E206. Large intestine - dryness of the colon
E207. Large intestine - Yang deficiency (cold)
E208. Heart - Blood insufficiency
E209. Heart - Blood stagnation
E210. Heart - Fire
E211. Heart - Hot mucus clogs the heart pores

E212. Heart - Cold mucus clogs the heart pores
E213. Heart - Qi deficiency
E214. Heart - Yang deficiency
E215. Heart - Yin deficiency
E216. Liver - Ascending Liver Yang
E217. Liver - Blood deficiency
E218. Liver - Blood stagnation
E219. Liver - Moisture heat in liver and gall bladder
E220. Liver - Fire
E221. Liver - Gall bladder Qi-Empty
E222. Liver - Cold in the liver meridian
E223. Liver - Qi stagnation
E224. Liver - Wind
E225. Liver - Wind with ascending liver Yang
E226. Liver - Wind with blood anemic
E227. Liver - Wind with extreme heat
E228. Lung - Qi deficiency
E229. Lung - Mucus-moisture in the lungs
E230. Lung - Mucus-heat in the lungs
E231. Lung - Mucus-cold in the lungs
E232. Lung - Dryness of the lungs
E233. Lung - Wind-heat attacks the lungs
E234. Lung - Wind-cold affects the lungs
E235. Lung - Yin deficiency
E236. Stomach - Bloodstagnation
E237. Stomach - Fire
E238. Stomach - Cold with liquid
E239. Stomach - Nutrition stagnation
E240. Stomach - Qi deficiency
E241. Stomach - Rebellious Qi
E242. Stomach - Yin Emptiness
E243. Spleen - Heat and moisture attack the spleen
E244. Spleen - Coldness and moisture affects the spleen
E245. Spleen - Qi deficiency
E246. Spleen - Qi deficiency + Declining spleen Qi
E247. Spleen - Qi deficiency + spleen does not control the blood
E248. Spleen - Yang deficiency
E249. Kidney - Heart and kidney no longer communicate
E250. Kidney - Jing deficiency
E251. Kidney - Kidneys cannot receive the Qi
E252. Kidney - Qi is not stable
E253. Kidney - Yang deficiency
E254. Kidney - Yin deficiency

For further information visit di-book.com.